Growing Readers

Purchased with Smart Start Funds

Thoughts and Feelings

Thoughts *and* Feelings

Frustrated

Written by Sylvia Root Tester
Photos by David M. Budd

The Child's World®, Inc.

Published by The Child's World®, Inc.

Design and Production:
The Creative Spark, San Juan Capistrano, CA

Photos: © 1998 David M. Budd Photography

Library of Congress Cataloging-in-Publication Data

Tester, Sylvia Root, 1939–
    Frustrated / by Sylvia Root Tester.
        p. cm. — (Thoughts and feelings)
    Includes bibliographical references.
    Summary: A child talks about how it feels to be frustrated and what
she does about it.
    ISBN 1-56766-668-X (lib. bdg. : alk. paper)
    1. Frustration in children—Juvenile literature. [1. Frustration.] I. Title.
II. Series.
BF723.F7T47   1999
152.4'7—dc21   99-25379
                                                                             CIP

Today was a day when everything went wrong! My coat wouldn't zip...

7

8

my pants were too long.

I couldn't get
my laces tied tight.

My sister
wanted to
pick a fight.

All day long
everything that I did
frustrated me!
Oh yes it did!

Do you know what the word

FRUST

means?

RATED

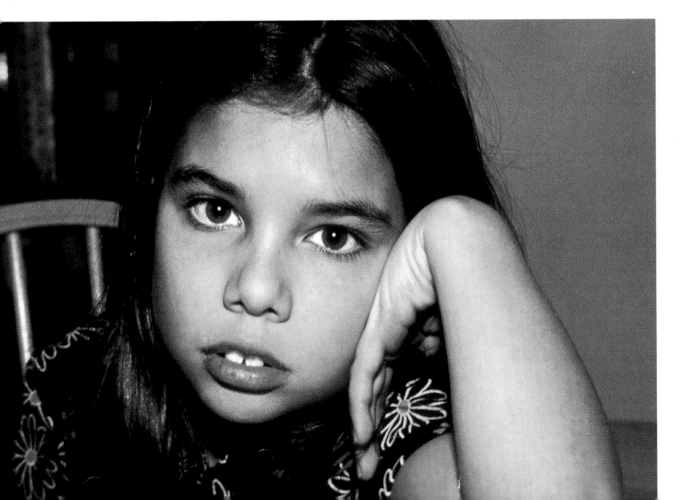

It's spilling pop on your top and your jeans.

20

It's having your ice cream
fall on the floor.

Or when your hands are too full to open the door.

It's playing and jumping
high in the air,
and landing KERPLUNK
while other kids stare.

It's trying to walk
your favorite dog,
who wants to stay put—
just like a log!

It's calling a friend
who isn't there.
"Frustrated" is more than
I think I can bear!

So I'll tell my mom about
my frustrating day.
I know she will help me.
She'll know what to say!
When you get frustrated
and don't know what to do,

try sharing your problems,
and let someone help you.　　31

For Further Information and Reading

Books

Crary, Elizabeth. *I'm Frustrated.* Seattle, WA: 1992.

Oram, Hiawyn. *Badger's Bad Mood.* New York: Scholastic Trade, 1998.

Viorst, Judith. *Alexander and the Terrible, Horrible, No Good, Very Bad Day.* New York: Athenium, 1972.

Web Sites

Dealing with Anger: How to Keep Your Cool:
http://www.kidshealth.org/kid/feeling/anger.html

What Is Stress?
http://www.kidshealth.org/kid/feeling/stress.html

Fairy tales and stories about thoughts and feelings from all over the world: http://www.familyinternet.com/StoryGrowby/